VERSAILLES
VISITOR'S GUIDE

DANIEL MEYER
CONSERVATEUR EN CHEF

art lys

Editorial co-ordination:
Denis Kilian
Layout: Aline Hudelot,
Marie-Blanche Baschet
Plans: Thierry Lebreton,
Dominique Bissière
Production: Pierre Kegels
Picture research: Christian Ryo
The text was edited by Christian Ryo

Photo credits:
RMN/Lewandowski
RMN/G. Blot
Artephot/Varga
art lys/E. Burnier
art lys/J. Girard
art lys/ P. Néri
art lys/Ch. Gœury

The Chateau

The Gardens

Trianon

Introduction

Versailles is known throughout the world as the largest and most sumptuous palace ever built. In the mind of the visitor unfamiliar with the twists and turns of the history of France, the names of Louis XIV and Marie Antoinette are jumbled up together, and the other kings, queens and princes who lived here are too often neglected. In their enthusiasm for an over-elaborated symbolism developed only after the event, certain authors have attempted to explain Versailles as an expression of the solar myth, on the pretext that Louis XIV was known as the Sun King (many of his forebears had been called the same thing), and that his bedchamber was placed at the geometrical centre of the chateau (which was a result of the re-working of the Royal Apartments in 1700).

In reality, the importance of Versailles and its inhabitants must be sought elsewhere. Rather than a solar symbol, Versailles was the symbol of the monarchy called the Ancien Régime, sometimes termed the absolute monarchy, which would however be better described as personal monarchy by divine right. Curiously, it was at Versailles, in a hunting-lodge soon to be replaced by a small chateau, during the Journée des Dupes in 1630, that Louis XIII confirmed Cardinal Richelieu in his powers, wholly possessed of royal authority just as had been Henri IV, the first king to come and hunt in the woods of Versailles. It was at Versailles in 1789 that the Estates General met for the last time, and the ancient Capetian monarchy which had ruled over France since 987 began its death agony.

Between 1630 and 1789 the chateau grew and its park developed into its present form, while a new town was built alongside it. From Louis XIII's hunting-lodge, Louis XIV made a country house, which grew larger and larger and ever more impressive, and in April 1682 he decided to establish his capital at Versailles. Le Vau and later Hardouin-Mansart, his architects, Le Brun, his painter and Le Nôtre his landscape gardener all made their mark, but the King's influence was decisive. From his mother Anne of Austria and his grandmother Marie de Medici Louis XIV had inherited a taste for the plastic arts; from his father Louis XIII, whom he had hardly known, and of whom he was told little, he got his taste for music.

In 1715 he was succeeded by his great-grandson Louis XV, who made no changes to the architecture of the chateau until towards the end of his reign in 1770. He had nonethe-

less inherited his grandfather's artistic tastes, as is witnessed by the private apartments; his sense of the importance of secrecy in politics he had received from his Italian ancestors the Medici and the House of Savoy. It was precisely in his private apartments, away from the indiscretions of the Court, that the King called the Well-Beloved took some of his most important decisions. He did not however forget the Court ceremonial established by his predecessor, nor the family life he was recalled to by a somewhat neglected Queen and especially by his much-loved daughters.

Finally, Louis XVI, the grandson of Louis XV, whose reign was interrupted by the Revolution, inherited from his grandfather, Augustus of Saxony, King of Poland, his herculean strength; and from his Bourbon ancestors he got not only his great fondness for hunting, but also a marked interest in the sciences. Beside him, Marie-Antoinette, the daughter of the Duke of Lorraine who had become Emperor, and thus the grand-daughter of Monsieur, the brother of Louis XIV, and the famous Princess Palatine, marked Versailles with her love of music, which she inherited from the Hapsburgs of Austria as well as from Louis XIII.

To tour the chateau and gardens of Versailles is to traverse centuries of history, and of the history of art. To realise this it is enough to mention the names of only a few of the most eminent artists who were at some time connected with Versailles: without counting the many painters and sculptors who played a part in decorating the chateau and its gardens, Molière, Racine, Lully, La Fontaine and Delalande all presented performances of their most important works. This alliance between the arts and royal power was particularly fruitful during the reign of Louis XIV, but the habit was maintained by his successors, and world-wide fame gained by Versailles from the 18th-century onward attracted talents of every kind.

Not only does it offer us a history of 17th and 18th-century art, but a visit to Versailles will also give us a better understanding of the France of old.

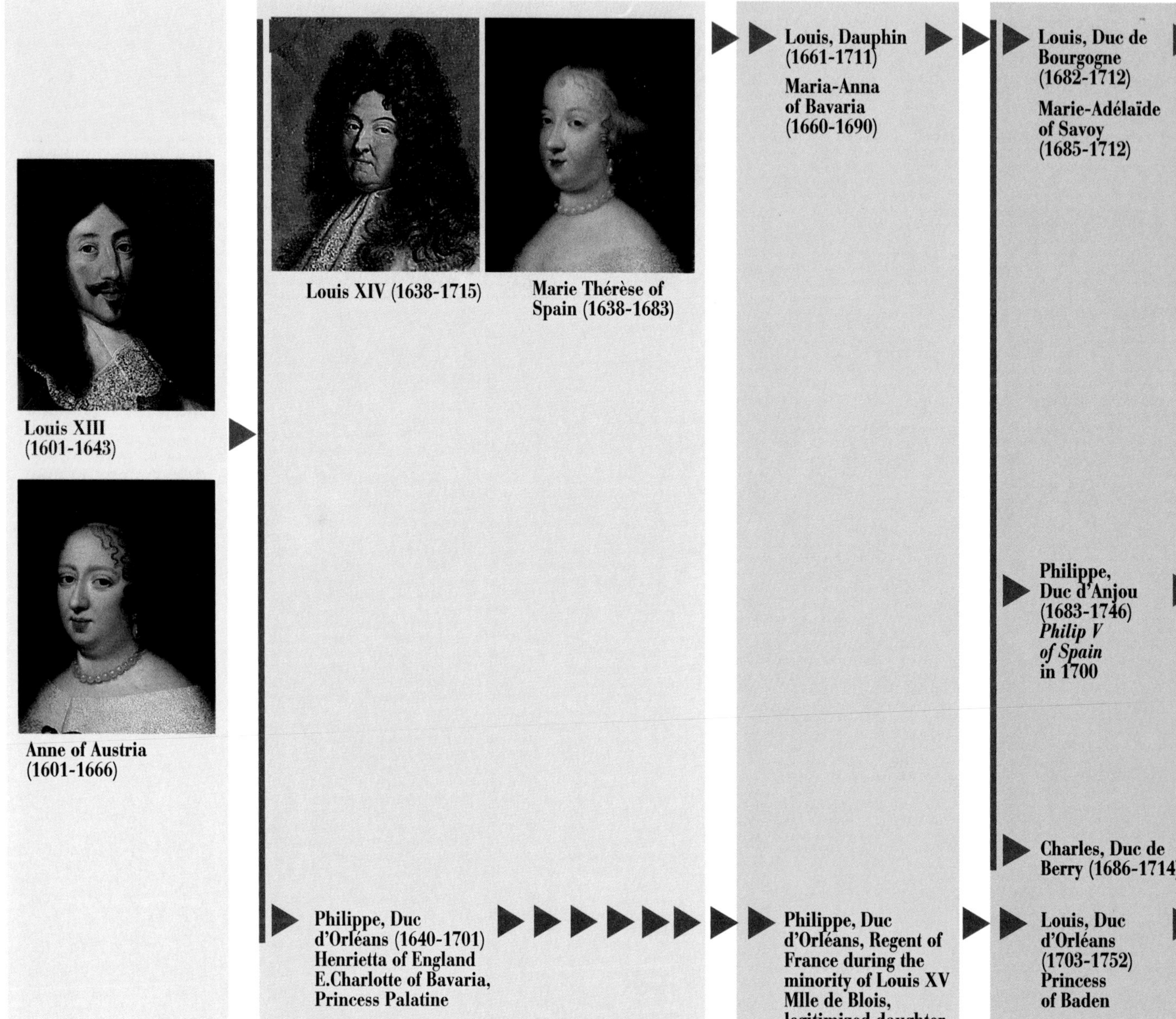

Chronology

1624 Louis XIII has a hunting-lodge built at Versailles.

1631 Louis XIII asks Philibert Le Roy to build a chateau on the site of the hunting-lodge.

1661 Death of Cardinal Mazarin the Prime Minister, and beginning of Louis XIV's personal reign. Colbert is appointed Superintendent of Finances. Birth of the Grand Dauphin.

1682 on May 6, Louis XIV orders that Versailles shall henceforth by the official residence of the Court and the seat of governement.

1684 Completion of the Hall of Mirrors. Constuction of Orangery.

1715 September 1, death of Louis XIV. September 9, Louis XV abandons Versailles for Vincennes.

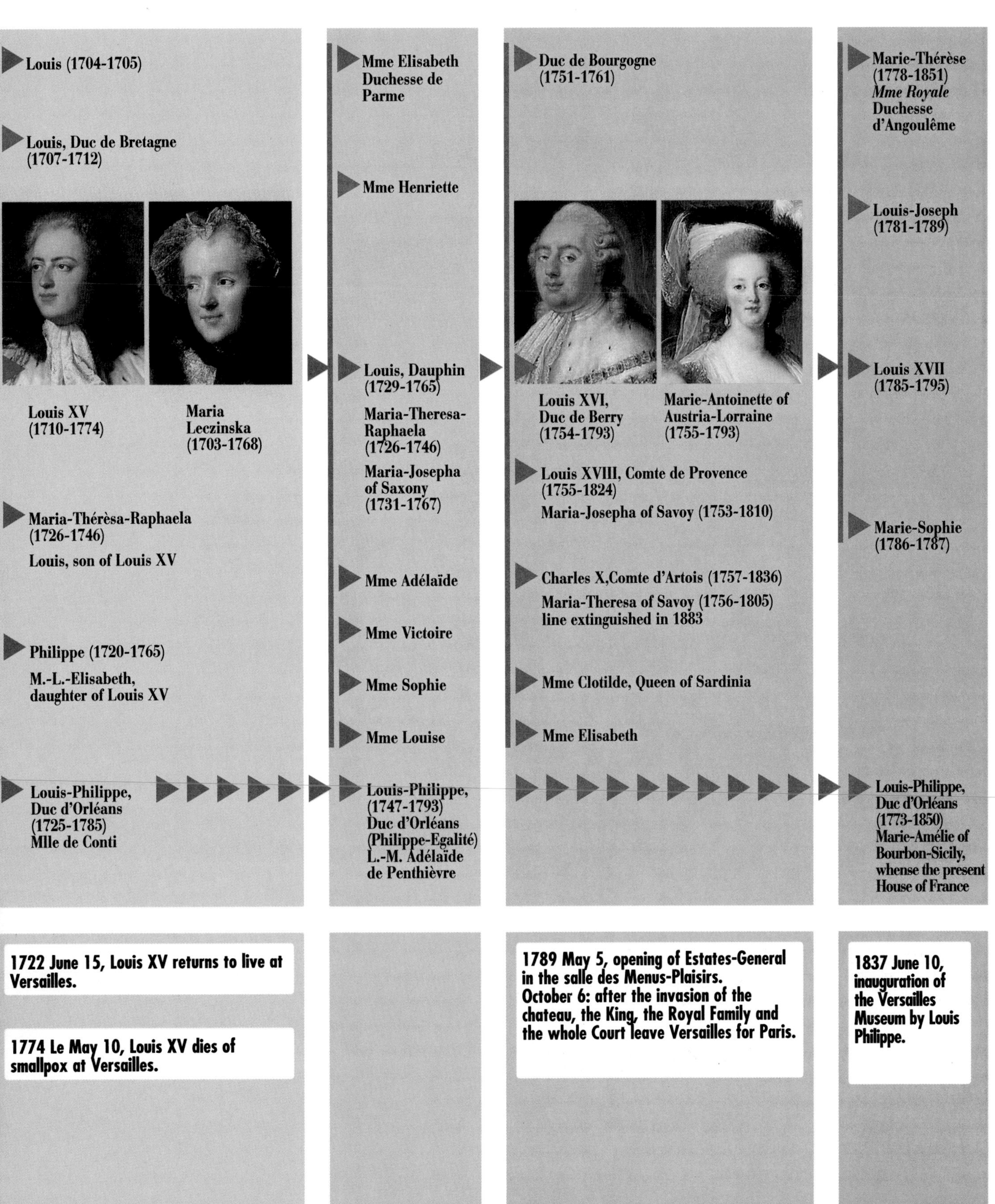
Louis (1704-1705)
Louis, Duc de Bretagne (1707-1712)
Louis XV (1710-1774)
Maria Leczinska (1703-1768)
Maria-Thérèsa-Raphaela (1726-1746)
Louis, son of Louis XV
Philippe (1720-1765)
M.-L.-Elisabeth, daughter of Louis XV
Louis-Philippe, Duc d'Orléans (1725-1785)
Mlle de Conti
Mme Elisabeth Duchesse de Parme
Mme Henriette
Louis, Dauphin (1729-1765)
Maria-Theresa-Raphaela (1726-1746)
Maria-Josepha of Saxony (1731-1767)
Mme Adélaïde
Mme Victoire
Mme Sophie
Mme Louise
Louis-Philippe, (1747-1793) Duc d'Orléans (Philippe-Egalité)
L.-M. Adélaïde de Penthièvre
Duc de Bourgogne (1751-1761)
Louis XVI, Duc de Berry (1754-1793)
Marie-Antoinette of Austria-Lorraine (1755-1793)
Louis XVIII, Comte de Provence (1755-1824)
Maria-Josepha of Savoy (1753-1810)
Charles X,Comte d'Artois (1757-1836)
Maria-Theresa of Savoy (1756-1805)
line extinguished in 1883
Mme Clotilde, Queen of Sardinia
Mme Elisabeth
Marie-Thérèse (1778-1851) *Mme Royale* Duchesse d'Angoulême
Louis-Joseph (1781-1789)
Louis XVII (1785-1795)
Marie-Sophie (1786-1787)
Louis-Philippe, Duc d'Orléans (1773-1850)
Marie-Amélie of Bourbon-Sicily, whense the present House of France
1722 June 15, Louis XV returns to live at Versailles.
1774 Le May 10, Louis XV dies of smallpox at Versailles.
1789 May 5, opening of Estates-General in the salle des Menus-Plaisirs.
October 6: after the invasion of the chateau, the King, the Royal Family and the whole Court leave Versailles for Paris.
1837 June 10, inauguration of the Versailles Museum by Louis Philippe.

General Plan of the Versailles Estate
1 The South Parterre
2 The Orangery
3 The Water Parterre
4 The Latona Fountain and Parterre
5 The North and South Quincunxes
6 The Bosquet des Rocailles
7 The Queen's Grove
8 The Mirror Pond and the King's Garden
9 The Fountain of Autumn
10 The Fountain of Winter
11 The Salle des Marroniers
12 The Colonnade
13 The Royal Avenue or Tapis Vert
14 The Fountain of Apollo and the Grand Canal
15 The Fountain of Enceladus
16 The Bosquet des Dômes
17 The Obelisk
18 The Fountain of Spring
19 The Fountain of Summer
20 The Bosquet de l'Etoile (Star Grove)
21 The Children's Island and the Rond Vert
22 The Baths of Apollo
23 The North Parterre
24 The Pyramid and Bathing Nymphs
25 The Water Avenue
26 The Dragon Fountain
27 The Fountain of Neptune
GRAND CANAL

28 The Grand Trianon
29 The Petit Trianon
30 The French Pavilion
31 The Belvedere
32 The Great Lake and the Hamlet
33 The Farm
34 The Queen's Cottage
35 The Mill
36 The Temple of Love

Ground-floor Plan of the Chateau

The Dauphine's Apartment
1 First Antechamber
2 Second Antechamber
3 State Cabinet
4 Bedchamber
5 Private Cabinet
6 Private Rooms of the Duchesse d'Angoulême

The Dauphin's Apartment
7 Library
8 State Cabinet
9 Bedchamber
10 Private Rooms
11 Second Antechamber
12 Galerie basse (Lower Gallery)

Madame Victoire's Apartment
13 First Antechamber
14 Salon des Nobles
15 State Cabinet
16 Bedchamber
17 Private Cabinet
18 Library

Madame Adélaïde's Apartment
19 Private Cabinet
20 Bedchamber
21 State Cabinet
22 Salle des Hocquetons (Archers' Room) formerly the antechambers to the apartment, and drawing-room of the Ambassadors' Staircase
23 Vestibule to the Ambassadors' Staircase
24 Vestibule
25 Room of the King's Guard
26 King's Staircase

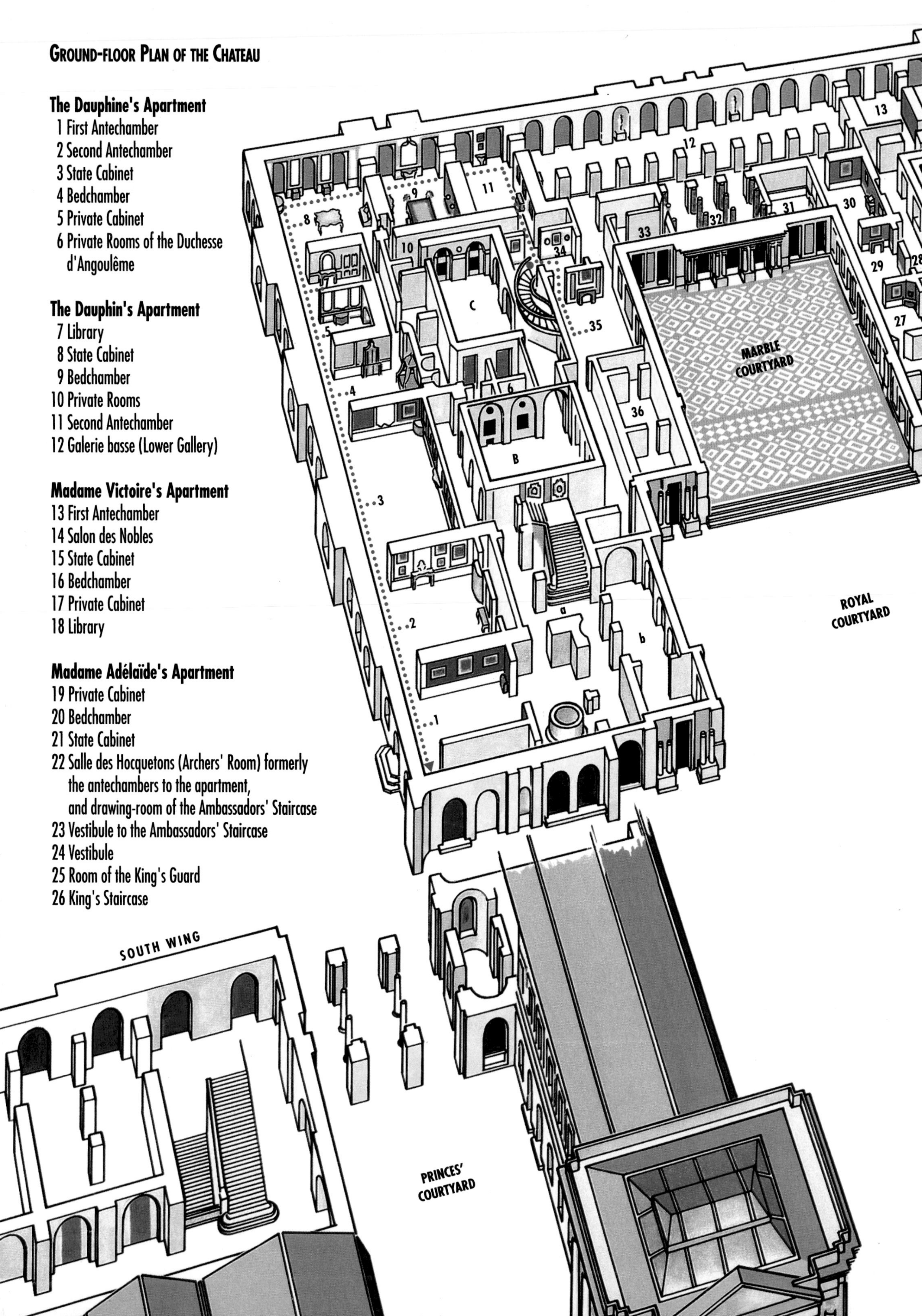

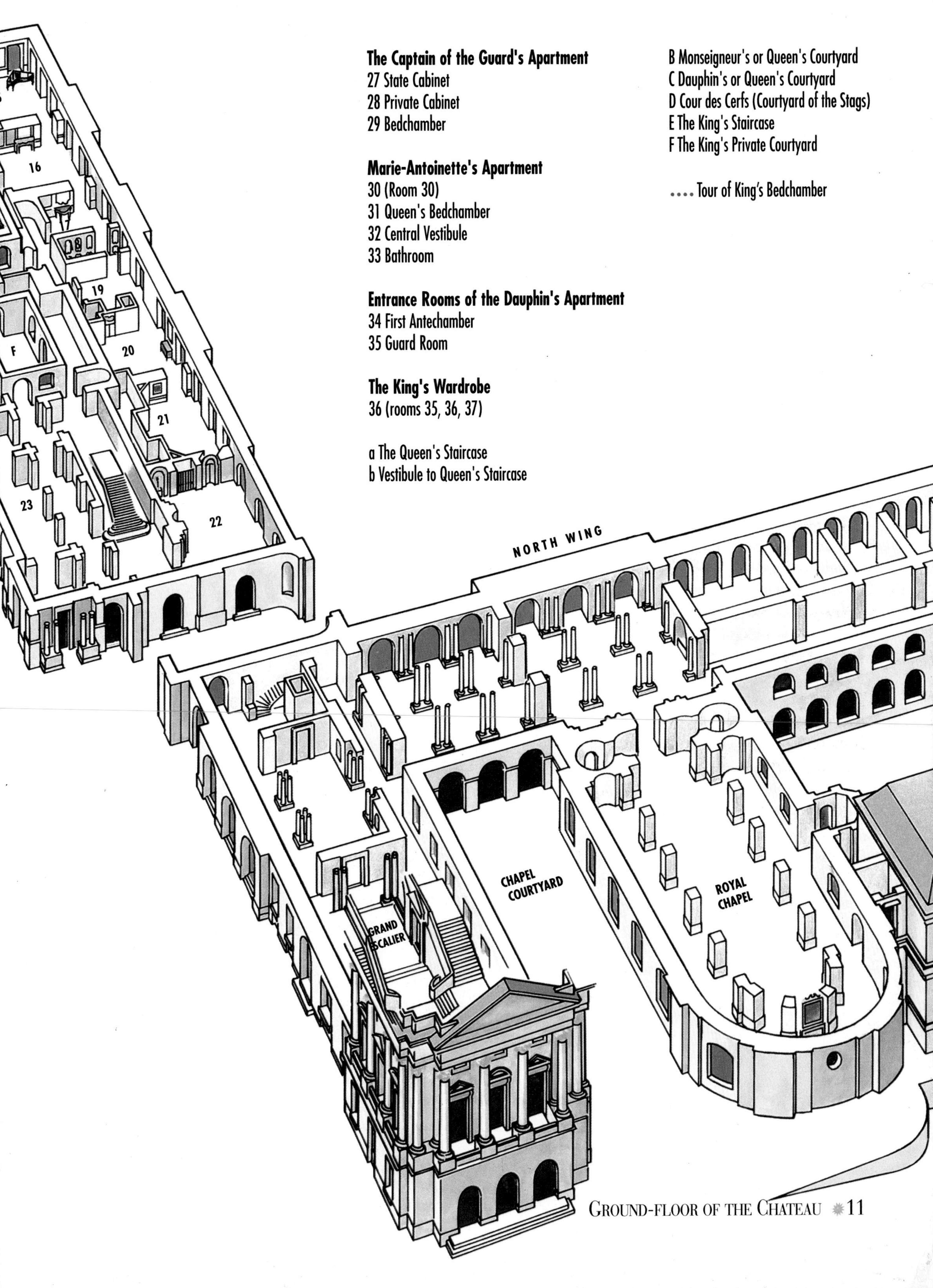
The Captain of the Guard's Apartment
27 State Cabinet
28 Private Cabinet
29 Bedchamber
Marie-Antoinette's Apartment
30 (Room 30)
31 Queen's Bedchamber
32 Central Vestibule
33 Bathroom
Entrance Rooms of the Dauphin's Apartment
34 First Antechamber
35 Guard Room
The King's Wardrobe
36 (rooms 35, 36, 37)
a The Queen's Staircase
b Vestibule to Queen's Staircase
B Monseigneur's or Queen's Courtyard
C Dauphin's or Queen's Courtyard
D Cour des Cerfs (Courtyard of the Stags)
E The King's Staircase
F The King's Private Courtyard
.... Tour of King's Bedchamber
16
19
20
21
22
23
F
NORTH WING
CHAPEL COURTYARD
ROYAL CHAPEL
GRAND ESCALIER

First-floor Plan of the Chateau

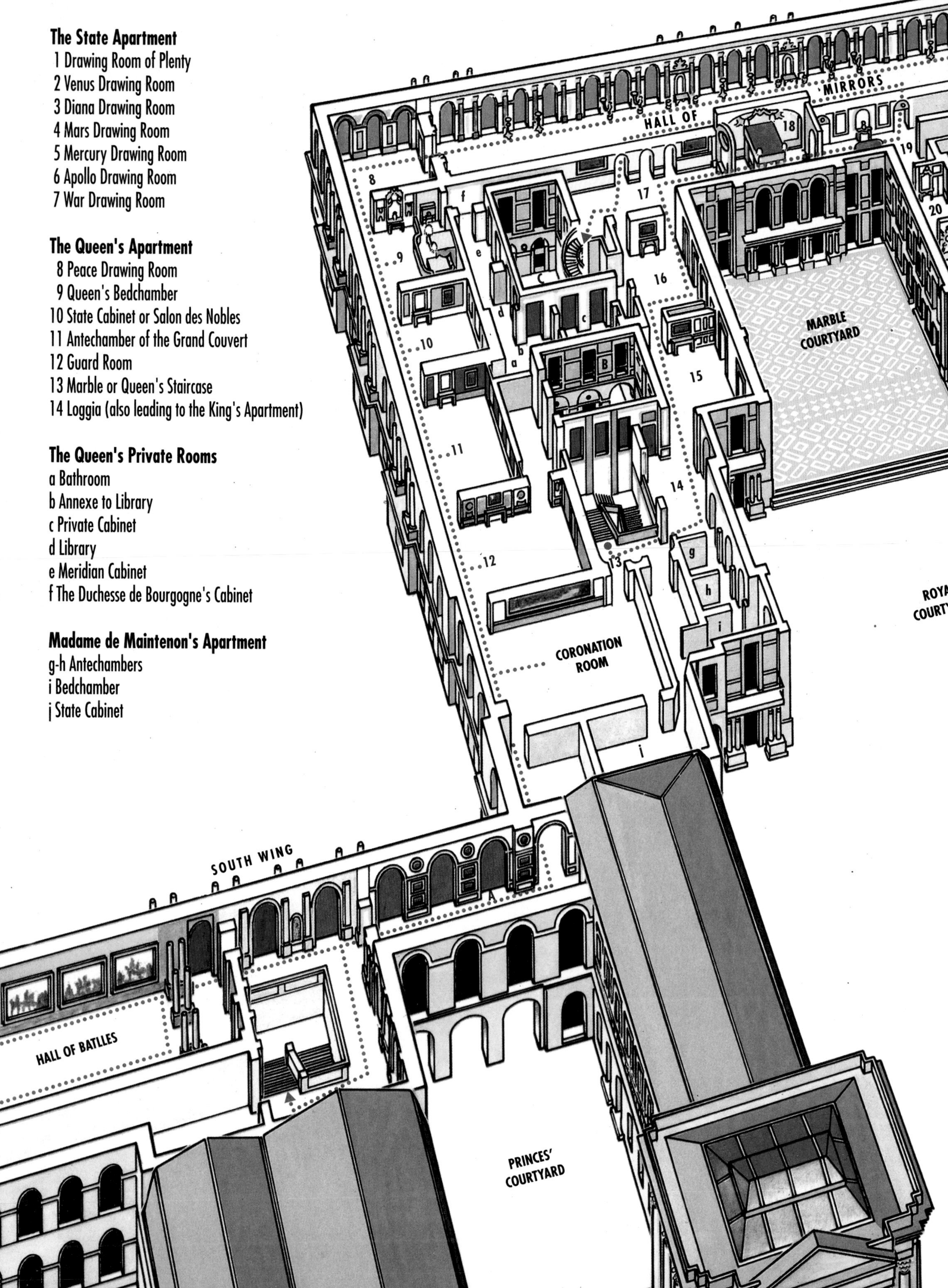

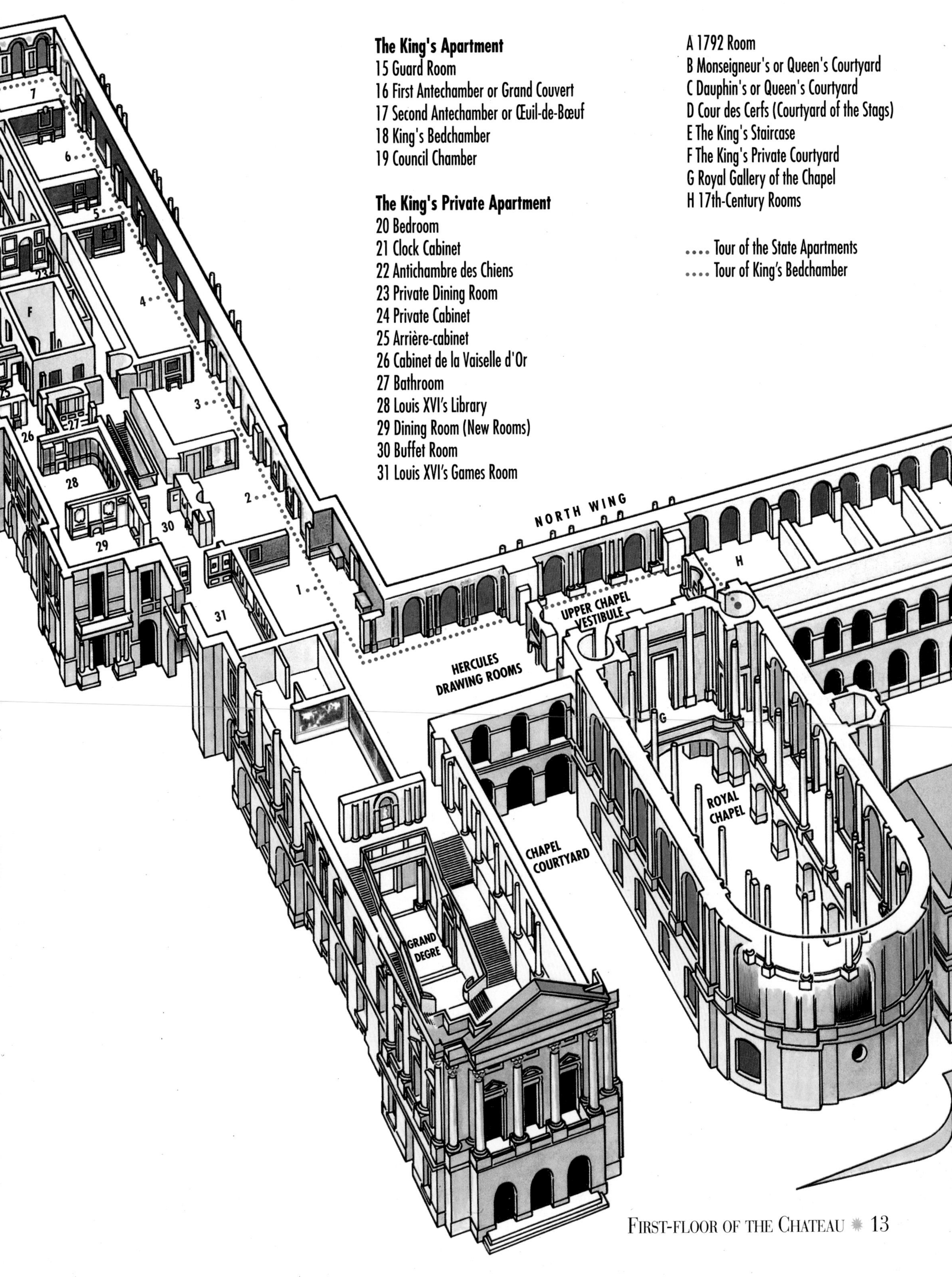
The King's Apartment
15 Guard Room
16 First Antechamber or Grand Couvert
17 Second Antechamber or Œuil-de-Bœuf
18 King's Bedchamber
19 Council Chamber
The King's Private Apartment
20 Bedroom
21 Clock Cabinet
22 Antichambre des Chiens
23 Private Dining Room
24 Private Cabinet
25 Arrière-cabinet
26 Cabinet de la Vaisselle d'Or
27 Bathroom
28 Louis XVI's Library
29 Dining Room (New Rooms)
30 Buffet Room
31 Louis XVI's Games Room
A 1792 Room
B Monseigneur's or Queen's Courtyard
C Dauphin's or Queen's Courtyard
D Cour des Cerfs (Courtyard of the Stags)
E The King's Staircase
F The King's Private Courtyard
G Royal Gallery of the Chapel
H 17th-Century Rooms
Tour of the State Apartments
Tour of King's Bedchamber
NORTH WING
UPPER CHAPEL VESTIBULE
HERCULES DRAWING ROOMS
ROYAL CHAPEL
CHAPEL COURTYARD
GRAND DEGRE

The Courtyards

Before entering the grounds of the chateau itself, the visitor has to cross the *Place d'Armes* (Royal Parade Ground), on which converge the three great avenues that traverse the town.

A view of Versailles in 1722 by Pierre-Denis Martin.

This painting by Pierre-Denis Martin makes it easy to grasp the ordered succession of different courtyards under the *Ancien Régime*. Beyond the gateway, crowned with the arms of France, lies the Great Courtyard. Since 1837 an equestrian statue of Louis XIV has stood where, before the Revolution, a second set of railings marked off the Royal Courtyard.

In the pediment abov the windows lookin over the Marbl Courtyard is a cloc whose hands wer once set to the hou of death of th previous king

The Marble Courtyard and the buildings alongside it are a reminder of the little chateau built by Louis XIII. His son refused to pull down this hunting-lodge as he had been advised to do by his architects, which therefore survives around this courtyard which Louis XIV was happy simply to embellish. The first floor is entirely occupied by the King's Apartments.

Only Princes, Marshals of France and Ambassadors were allowed to enter the Royal Courtyard in their carriages.

The Royal Chapel

Following the model of the Palatine chapels, the Royal Chapel has two storeys. The galleries were reserved for the King, the royal family and important members of the Court, and connected directly to the State Apartment on the same floor. The rest of the congregation occupied the ground floor.

Consecrated in 1710, and dedicated to Saint Louis, ancestor and patron saint of the royal family, the chapel was the last building to be constructed at Versailles in the reign of Louis XIV. It followed four temporary chapels established each in its turn at the heart of the chateau. The plans presented to the King by Jules Hardouin-Mansart were approved in 1699, and when the architect died, his brother-in-law Robert Cotte took over the work.

Designed by Robert de Cotte, the high altar is the work of Corneille van Clève, who sculpted the glory surrounding Jehovah.

The decoration of the ceiling depicts the continuity between Old and New Testaments, with its three constituent paintings referring to the Holy Trinity: in the centre, *The Glory of the Father Announcing the Coming of the Messiah,* by Antoine Coypel; above the altar, *The Resurrection of Christ,* by Charles de Lafosse; and above the Royal Gallery, *The Holy Spirit Descending upon the Virgin and the Apostles,* by Jean Jouvenet.

The Chapel Drawing Room

To attend Mass the King had to cross this room, which links the Royal Gallery to the State Apartment. Its decoration is therefore related to that of the chapel, but the themes are more secular; in addition to the ornamentation of the arches above doors and windows, two niches hold statues commissioned by Louis XV: *Glory holding the Medallion of Louis XV,* by Vassé, and *Royal Magnanimity,* by Bousseau.

The organ indicates the important role of music in religious ceremonies; the greatest musicians of the reign of Louis XIV performed their works here, in particular Michel Richard Delalande, appointed under-choirmaster at Versailles in 1683.

A connecting room essentially leading from one place to another, the Hercules Drawing Room was little furnished, but on account of its size it was used under the *Ancien Régime* for concerts and full-dress balls and for the reception of ambassadors.

THE HERCULES DRAWING ROOM

Begun in 1712 by Robert de Cotte, work was interrupted on the death of the Sun King in 1715, and finished only in 1736 with the completion of François Lemoine's ceiling representing *The Apotheosis of Hercules.* This painting, which took three years to finish (from 1733 to 1736) made him famous and earned him the title of First Painter to the King.

To complete the decor in rare marbles, which matches the colour-scheme of Veronese's painting, above the fireplace there stands another painting by the same artist, depicting *The Meeting of Eliezer and Rebecca.*

Built as a setting for Veronese's *Meal at the House of Simon the Pharisee*, a gift to Louis XIV from the Republic of Venice in 1664, this is the largest drawing room in the chateau.

The Ambassadors' Staircase

Destroyed in 1752, the Ambassadors' Staircase led to the State Apartment.

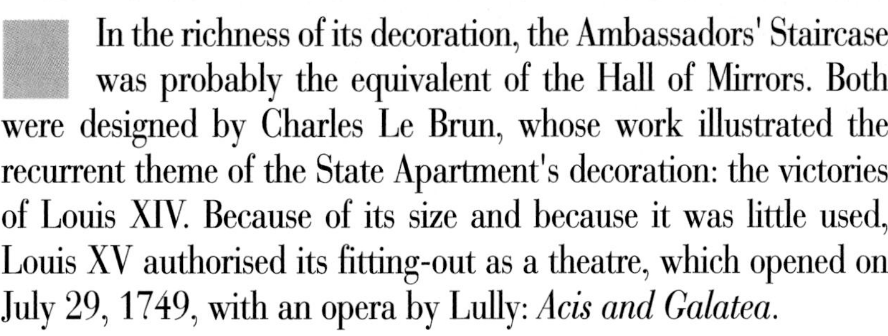

In the richness of its decoration, the Ambassadors' Staircase was probably the equivalent of the Hall of Mirrors. Both were designed by Charles Le Brun, whose work illustrated the recurrent theme of the State Apartment's decoration: the victories of Louis XIV. Because of its size and because it was little used, Louis XV authorised its fitting-out as a theatre, which opened on July 29, 1749, with an opera by Lully: *Acis and Galatea*.

THE DRAWING ROOM OF PLENTY 1

On "Apartment" evenings, courtiers would come here for to refresh themselves at the three great buffets where drinks were served. "Apartment evenings" was the name for the entertainments offered by the King to his courtiers on Monday, Wednesday and Thursday evenings, from six till ten.

Thanks to the balustrade painted around the ceiling by Houasse, we have some idea of the objects contained in Louis XIV's Cabinet of Curios and Rare Objects. The most marvellous was the nef decorated with diamonds and rubies which held the King's napkin and cutlery, and which is depicted above the door, opposite the windows. Above the balustrade, the ceiling shows *Royal Munificence*.

At first, this drawing room gave onto the Cabinet of Curios and Rare Objects (today Louis XIV's Games Room), where were exhibited the most precious items from Louis XIV's collections. According to Mademoiselle de Scudéry, they were "vessels set with gold, with diamonds; others with agates encrusted with emeralds, turquoise, jade, pearls etc., Chinese and Japanese porcelain".

THE VÉNUS 2
[DR]AWING ROOM.

On "Apartment" evenings, the Venus Drawing Room was used for the serving of light meals. The *Mercure Galant* reports that tables were set up there spread with silver dishes containing preserves and fresh and crystallized fruit.

In the ceiling oval, René-Antoine Houasse painted the subject which gives this drawing room its name, *The Goddess of Love subjugating the Gods and Powers.*

In 1752, the Ambassadors' Staircase, which until then had provided access to the State Apartment, and whose sumptuous decor had so impressed the visitor, was destroyed. The Venus and Diana Drawing Rooms still retain the marble decor which matched that of the staircase, to which they served as upper vestibules.

Glorification of the sovereign here takes the form of a full-length statue by Jean Warin representing Louis XIV as a Roman emperor.

The Diana Drawing Room 3

The whole of the decoration of this room refers to the legend of the goddess Diana. Above the fireplace is the Charles de Lafosse's *Sacrifice of Iphigenia,* and opposite is *Diana Watching over the Sleeping Endymion* (1672) by Gabriel Blanchard.

Bust of Louis XIV by Bernini.

Louis XIV, who was an excellent billiard-player, had a large table set up here, covered when not in use with a crimson velvet cloth, its edges fringed with gold. The ladies followed the game from benches set up on platforms, which gave them a good view and allowed them to applaud the King's successes.

The Mars Drawing Room 4

Until 1682, this was used as a guardroom, which explains its name, and in particular the cornice alternately decorated with helmets and trophies.
It then changed its function, being used for concerts on "Apartment" evenings, and between 1684 and 1750 there were galleries for musicians on either side of the chimney-breast.

Domenichino's *David*, which in 1794 is mentioned as being in the neighbouring Mercury Drawing Room, has been placed where during the reign of Louis XIV there hung Veronese's *Mystic Marriage of Saint Catherine.*

In 1682, when Court and Government were officially established at Versailles, the Mercury Drawing Room was the State Bedchamber, furnished with a bed embroidered in gold. On "Apartment" evenings it was reserved for the royal family's games. Games were very popular at Versailles, and were intended to amuse the court. They were sometimes played for money, and some courtiers did not hesitate to stake large sums.

This room also witnessed less happy occasions, and for a week following the death of Louis XIV on September 2, 1715, seventy-two priests took turns to pray here, the room transformed into a candle-lit mortuary chapel.

The Mercury Drawing Room 5

The Mercury and Apollo Drawing Rooms were the most luxurious in the chateau of Versailles, but none of the silver furniture from the reign of Louis XIV survives. It is therefore difficult to imagine their grandeur in the days of the *Ancien Régime*.

The automaton clock was a gift to Louis XIV by the clock-maker Antoine Morand in 1706. When the hour strikes, there appear the figures of Louis XIV and of Fame descending from a cloud.

The central motif of the ceiling painted by Jean-Baptiste de Champaigne shows *Mercury in his Chariot Drawn by Two Cocks*. The same artist painted the ceiling-coves representing *Alexander the Great and Ptolemy II surrounded by Scholars and Philosophers*.

THE APOLLO DRAWING ROOM 6

On "Apartment" evenings the Apollo Drawing Room cast off its official character to welcome music and dancing. The King himself took part in these entertainments.

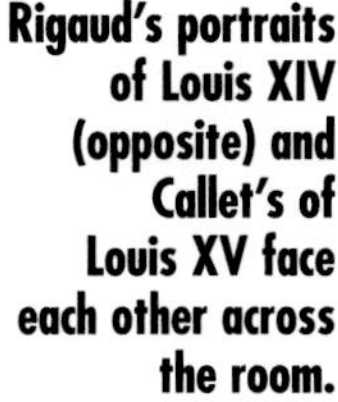

Rigaud's portraits of Louis XIV (opposite) and Callet's of Louis XV face each other across the room.

The Apollo Drawing Room was the Throne Room. On the end wall can still be seen the eye-bolts used to fasten the daïs which supported the eight-foot high silver throne used by Louis XIV until 1689. Here the King received ambassadors in formal audience. Extraordinary audiences were held in the Hall of Mirrors.

THE WAR DRAWING ROOM 7

The War Drawing Room evokes Louis XIV's victories over the allied powers (The Empire, Spain and Holland) during the war with Holland, and the Peace of Nijmegen which brought it to an end in 1678.

The War Drawing Room, the Hall of Mirrors and the Peace Drawing Room form an ensemble whose decor is devoted to the military victories and political successes of Louis XIV.

In collaboration with Le Conte, Arcy and Prou, Coysevox executed the trophies which surmount the mirrored false doors, reflecting the same spirit as the bas-reliefs of the fireplace.

The Hall of Mirrors is not contemporary with the first works carried out by the architect Le Vau. In the plan for a stone envelope around Louis XIII's little chateau, its place was occupied by a terrace. It was Jules Hardouin-Mansart who on September 26, 1678, (the year of the Peace of Nijmegen) presented the King with plans for the construction of the present Hall of Mirrors. Work began immediately, and was completed in 1686.

The chimney-piece, designed by Le Brun, is decorated with bas-reliefs by Antoine Coysevox. The large medallion portrays an important episode of the war with Holland: Louis XIV is represented on horseback in classical dress on the occasion of the French troops' crossing of the Rhine on June 12, 1672. On the fireplace one sees Clio, the muse of History, writing the history of the King.

The Hall of Mirrors

Under the *Ancien Régime* the Hall of Mirrors functioned as a passageway giving access to the King's Apartment. Here gathered the courtiers who hoped to see the monarch when each morning he made his way to the Chapel. Some took the opportunity to present some request. When he received extraordinary embassies, such as that of Siam in 1686, Louis XIV would have the silver throne moved here from its usual place in the Apollo Drawing Room. Grand celebrations were also held here, such as, for example, full-dress balls, and the masked balls given on the occasion of princely marriages.

At first, Louis XIV had the Hall of Mirrors furnished with pieces in solid silver designed by Charles Le Brun. But these were melted down in 1689 to meet the expenses of war. These original fittings were candelabra, pedestal tables, and tables for torches, great vases to hold orange-trees, all finely worked by the finest silversmiths of the time. The present fixtures are replicas of those commissioned by Louis XV in 1770 for the wedding of his grandson the future Louis XVI to Marie-Antoinette.

In his ceiling-painting, Le Brun portrayed the history of Louis XIV's reign, and its central theme is the war against Holland and its allies (1672-1678) and the War of Devolution (1667-1668).
The whole composition is organised around a central motif entitled *The King Governs Alone,* in which one sees Louis XIV, face to face with the great European powers, turn away from his games and pleasures to contemplate the crown of immortality held out to him by Glory, and which is pointed out to him by Mars, god of war.

The King orders the attack on Holland in 1672; by Charles Le Brun.

8 The Peace Drawing Room

Because of its closeness to the Queen's Apartment, this drawing room was used as the Queen's Games Room. Here, every Sunday, Louis XV's wife Maria Leczinska gave concerts of sacred and secular music which played an important role in the musical life of Versailles.

As its name suggests, the decoration of this drawing room is dedicated to peace: the peace which followed the wars represented in the War Drawing Room and the Hall of Mirrors, and that established by the Kings of France as an expression of France's dominant place in Europe.

Above the fireplace is a painting by François Lemoine (1729), showing Louis XV offering Europe an olive-branch.

The Queen's Apartment

The characteristic symmetry which marks Versailles existed from the beginning between the Queens Apartment and the King's. Both had the same number of rooms, the decoration of the ceilings was devoted to the same divinities and planets, and they differed only in the paintings of the ceiling-coves, which in the King's Apartment portrayed male, and in the Queen's, female figures.

The Queen's Bedchamber 9

Governed by etiquette, most of the Queen's daily life was spent in her bedchamber. Here she granted audiences to the most important personages of the court, or to foreigners of standing who were visiting Versailles.

The original decor was designed by Charles Le Brun for Queen Maria-Theresa, but nothing of it survives. The present painted and sculpted decoration is that carried out for Maria Leczinska between 1730 and 1735.
Above the doors are portraits of her children, of whom there were then five (she would go on to have ten).
The furnishings are what Marie-Antoinette would have known: that is to say the "summer furnishings" which were up in the room when on October 6, 1789, the revolutionary mob forced the royal family to leave Versailles for good and take up residence at the Tuileries.

The two doors covered by hangings lead to the Queen's Private Cabinets, fifteen or so small rooms reserved for the Queen's private life and for the practicalities of waiting upon her. It is through the left-hand door that Marie-Antoinette fled to escape the rioters who had invaded her apartment.

It was in this room, in public. that the Queen, gave birth to the heirs to the throne. In her *Memoirs*, Madame de Campan, who was Marie-Antoinette's First Woman of the Bedchamber, described what such a birth could be like: "the moment that Vermond the accoucheur announced `The Queen is about to give birth', the crowds of spectators who rushed into her room were so numerous and disorderly that one thought the Queen would perish... Two Savoyards got up on the furniture the more easily to see the Queen, who was facing the fireplace on a bed got ready for her labour."

Meridian Cabinet

The Queen's Private Cabinet

In her Private Cabinet, completed in 1783, Marie-Antoinette received such people as her favourite painter, Madame Vigée-Lebrun, and the composer Gluck, her old music-teacher, but also Mlle Bertin, her dress-maker by appointment.

In her *Memoirs*, Madame Campan, Marie-Antoinette's First Woman of the Bedchamber, tells us something about the function of these private rooms: "The list of people received in the Queen's private rooms had been given to the Ushers of the Bedchamber by the Princess de Lamballe, and the people listed there could avail themselves of this favour only on days when the Queen desired the company of her intimates, which was only after child-birth or when she was slightly indisposed. Persons of the first rank at Court would sometimes ask her for private audiences; the Queen would then receive them in the room preceded by what was called the room of the ladies-in-waiting, who announced the arrival of visitors to the Queen's private rooms."

10 The Salon des Nobles

In the Salon des Nobles, the Queen of France held official audiences, and ladies newly admitted to Court were presented to her. For these ceremonies the Queen's armchair stood on a daïs, surmounted by a great canopy.

This room served first of all as an antechamber to Maria-Theresa's apartment, and then changed name and function to become successively the Queen's Drawing Room, and then the Queen's State Cabinet in the time of Maria Leczinska. Certain elements of the decor, the ceiling in particular, which portrays an allegory of Mercury, recall the fact that originally the Queen's Apartment was symmetrical with the King's.

Only the ceiling dates from the time of Maria-Theresa. Michel Corneille's painting portrays *Mercury Spreading his Influence over the Arts and the Sciences.*

In Queen Maria-Theresa's day, this room was the Room of the Queen's Guard, hence the ceiling decorated with warlike themes. It became an antechamber some years later, for the Dauphine, Maria-Anna of Bavaria, the daughter-in-law of Louis XIV. Visitors who had an audience with the Queen would bide their time here before entering the *Salon des Nobles* or the Bedchamber. It was also used for concerts and theatrical performances, making use of the little collapsible theatre installed in 1671. In 1701, during the pregnancy of the Dauphine, Marie-Adélaïde of Savoy, there were performances of Corneille's *Polyeucte* and Molière's *Misanthrope*.

ANTICHAMBER OF THE GRAND COUVERT 11

The name Grand Couvert comes from that of the ceremonial requiring that the King and Queen eat certain meals in public. One of the most notable was the meal that Louis XV and Maria Leczinska took here in the company of the young Mozart on January 1, 1764.

The paintings exhibited here are all the work of women painters of the 18th century: the two portraits of Marie-Antoinette by Elisabeth-Louise VigÈe-Lebrun, and the portraits of the daughters of Louis XV by Adélaïde Labille-Guiard.

12 The Guard Room

It was here that on the morning of October 6, 1789, guards lost their lives helping Marie-Antoinette seek refuge by the King's side.

This room, set aside for the use of the Queen's bodyguard, was always cluttered with racks for their arms, tables, and camp-beds hidden by screens. It was here that all the ladies of the court, except Princesses of the Blood, had to leave their sedan-chairs and their servants before going any further into the apartment.

In the corners of the ceiling, Noël Coypel painted the figures of courtiers leaning over into the room, watching the comings and goings.

Portrait of Maréchal Ney by F. Bataille. In the 1792 Room are portraits of the military heroes of the Revolution and the Empire

THE SALLE DU SACRE

Courtiers nicknamed this room, permanently cluttered with benches, screens, and the sedan chairs of the ladies of the court, the "magasin" or store-room. On Maundy Thursday, the King recalled the Last Supper by washing the feet of thirteen poor children. Today, the Salle du Sacre owes its name to the painting by David depicting the coronation of Napoleon I on December 2, 1804 (the first version is in the Louvre, and this one was completed in 1822).

At first this room was occupied by the chateau's third chapel. When in 1682 the Court and Government were officially established at Versailles, it served as the common guardroom of the King's and Queen's guards. They would meet here before taking up their posts in the chateau. All the paintings gathered here by Louis-Philippe when he turned the chateau into a museum in 1837 are devoted to the glorification of the Napoleonic era.

The work of the architects Neveu and Fontaine, this monumental space was part of Louis-Philippe's project for a museum of French history, intended to reconcile monarchists, republicans and Bonapartists. Vast paintings cover fourteen centuries of the history of France, from Clovis to Napoleon I.

The Hall of Battles

Situated on the first floor of the South Wing (or Princes' Wing), the Hall of Battles took the place of the apartments of the members of the royal family.

The Marble Staircase

The Marble Staircase, also called the Queen's Staircase, because at first it served only the Queen's Apartment, was also used to reach the King's Apartment after the death of his wife in 1683. It was designed as a worthy match for the Ambassadors' Staircase.

The King's Apartment

Antechamber of the *Grand Couvert*
Guard Room
Antechamber of the Œil-de-Boeuf
The King's Bedchamber
Council Chamber

Every Monday morning in the Antechamber of the *Grand Couvert*, a table was set out covered in green cloth, behind which the King was symbolically represented by an empty armchair: here courtiers could table their petitions.

At ten o'clock every evening Louis XIV took supper "au grand couvert", that is, in public and most often to music, and Michel-Richard Delalande wrote his *Symphonies for the King's Suppers* for this ritual occasion. The King's table stood before the fireplace, his spoon, his knife and his fork were brought in a box wrought of gold called the Cadenas. The food was prepared in a building called the Grand Commun more than two hundred metres away, and paraded with great pomp to the royal table.

The guardrooms were often used as "parking-lots", because courtiers were not allowed to enter into certain rooms, the King's Apartment in particular, with their sedan-chairs or servants.

A battle-scene with the King's Guards, by Joseph Parrocel.

The Antechamber of the Œil-de-Bœuf 17

Not everyone was received simultaneously at the ritual of the *Lever*, when the King rose from bed. The order of entry was prescribed by etiquette: first came the royal family, then the great officers of the Crown, then those who held an office at Court and finally the courtiers more generally.

Sparsely furnished, this vast room would be enlivened by the crowd of high-ranking courtiers who waited here hoping to be able to attend the King as he rose. It was here that intrigues and plots were made and unmade. Behaviour was governed by a strict etiquette, and one reads in 1694 that one should not bang loudly but scratch softly at the doors of the Bedchamber, the Antechamber or of the King's private rooms. If one wanted to leave, one could not open the door oneself, but had to have it done by the usher. The name of this second antechamber comes from the unusual bull's-eye window in the cornice of the room.

Louis XIV and the royal family, by Jean Nocret.

The King's Bedchamber 18

Of the important events which occurred in this room, the first was the death of Louis XIV on September 1, 1715. He had reigned for seventy-two years. On October 6, 1789, Louis XVI had to appear on the balcony with his family.

France watching over the sleep of the King.

At first, this was a state drawing-room which stood between the King's and Queen's apartments, and after the death of Louis XIV's wife, Maria-Theresa of Spain, it became the room "where the King dresses". It was only in 1701 that it became Louis XIV's bedchamber, where he would die on September 1, 1715. Then Louis XV stayed here until 1737; after this, and during the reign of Louis XVI, it was used only for the ceremonies of the *Lever and the Coucher*.

The Council Chamber 19

The Council of State met on Sundays and Wednesdays, and occasionally on Mondays, while the Council of Finances met on Tuesdays and Saturdays. Thursday was reserved for private audiences.

This room was only enlarged to its present size in the reign of Louis XV. In the time of his great-grandfather Louis XIV, two rooms occupied the same space. One was already a Council Chamber, while the other was the King's Wig Cabinet, where the King's wigs were stored in cupboards. This room reminds us that from 1682 Versailles was the seat of the government of France, and thus not only a place of entertainment but also a place of work.

The woodwork, carved by Rousseau to designs by Gabriel, evokes the King's various councils in war and peace.

THE KING'S PRIVATE APARTMENT:
AFTER-HUNT DINING ROOM
CLOCK CABINET
LOUIS XV'S BEDCHAMBER
PRIVATE CABINET

20 LOUIS XV'S BEDCHAMBER

In 1738, Louis XV had this bedroom installed, smaller and more comfortable than that in the King's "public" Apartment, which was now used only for the ceremonies of the Lever and the Coucher.

It was here that Louis XV died of smallpox on May 10, 1774. So that monarchical tradition should be respected, and the death of the sovereign take place in public despite the risk of infection, the dying Louis XV was brought here and laid on a camp-bed in the middle of the room, so that members of the Government and of the Court who were in the Council Chamber should be able to witness his death.

THE CLOCK CABINET 21

This room takes its name from the astronomical clock by Passamant, whose complex mechanism enables it to tell the time, the day of the week, the date in the month, the month, the year and the phase of the moon. Within the crystal globe above one can see the planets revolve around the sun according to Copernican principles. The brass line set into the floor marks the Versailles meridian.

The King's Private Apartment replaced the cabinets where Louis XIV had exhibited some of the finest pieces from his collections of medals, paintings, and objets d'art. Only a few visitors had the privilege of being invited by the King to visit this apartment. In 1738, Louis XV no longer wished to use his great-grandfather's bedchamber, and asked Gabriel to make alterations to this apartment to make it more comfortable.

In his Private Cabinet, which occupies part of what had been Louis XIV's Painting Cabinet, Louis XV found the peace to work alone or with one of his ministers.

24 The Private Cabinet

The most impressive piece of furniture is the roll-top desk, commissioned from the Oeben the cabinet-maker, who designed it and built the carcase, but who died in 1763 before completing his masterpiece. Riesener was then commissioned to produce the marquetry-work. It was only ten years after placing his order that Louis XV finally received his desk in 1769.

It was only in 1769 that Louis XV had the New Rooms added to the King's Private Apartment. These rooms had previously been Mme de Montespan's Apartment, then the *Petite Galerie*, then becoming an apartment for Madame Adélaïde, the daughter of Louis XV. Their present decor, however, essentially evokes the reign of Louis XVI.

The New Rooms

The library built for Louis XVI in 1774 contains a round table by Riesener whose top is made from a single piece of exotic hardwood 2.10 metres in diameter.

This porcelain plaque with its design painted after Jean-Baptiste Oudry's *Royal Hunts* was already part of the decor of the Porcelain Dining Room in the reign of Louis XV. The room takes its name from the annual exhibition of Sèvres porcelain which the King had organised here.

Louis XVI's Games Room is Louis XIV's old Medal Cabinet. The furniture is as it was on the eve of the Revolution.

The King's Private Cabinets

If Louis XIV believed that the existence of the sovereign should be public in its smallest details, this wasn't the case for his successors, who had rooms created for them which allowed for a more private life.

The King's Staircase was the scene of Damiens' famous attempt against the life of Louis XV on January 5, 1757.

Madame du Barry's Library.

The King's Private Cabinets is the name given to a suite of rooms above the King's Private Apartment which were the private space of Louis XV and Louis XVI. The library and its annexes, the Geography and Physics Cabinets, illustrate these kings' interest in scholarship and research. Some rooms became apartments for the King's intimates, and some of these have left their names attached to the "grace and favour" apartments that Louis XV provided for Mme du Barry, or Louis XVI for his minister Maurepas.

The Dauphin's Apartment

The Dauphin's Library, where Louis XV's son spent his time over books useful for the education of a future sovereign, contains a chest of drawers made for the apartment by Criaerd, and a desk by Gaudreaux made for Louis XV's Private Cabinet.

The globe in the State Cabinet was commissioned from the geographer Mantelle for the education of his son. It shows the oceans and the continents, and the heavens also are represented inside the first sphere.

After being the Work Cabinet of the Regent, who died there on December 2, 1723, this room was the bedchamber of the Dauphin, the son of Louis XV, and of the Dauphins, the sons of Louis XVI.

No trace has survived of the first occupants of the Dauphin's Apartment, the Duc d'Orléans, brother of Louis XIV, and his wife the Princess Palatine. There is more evidence of their successors, either in the form of portraits or in the form of furniture that belonged to them. These apartments are known as the Dauphin's and Dauphine's, after the eldest son of Louis XV and his wife Maria-Josepha of Saxony, the parents of Louis XV, Louis XVI and Charles X. These princes occupied the rooms from 1747 to 1765. It is from their time that there survive the most significant elements: the Dauphin's Bedchamber, his State Cabinet, his Library and the Dauphine's Private Cabinet.

THE PRIVATE CABINET 5

The original decor of unstained wood treated with "vernis Martin" designed by Jacques-Ange Gabriel in 1747 has survived in part, and was used as a model for the restoration of the whole room.

The Cup of Chocolate, by Jean Baptiste Charpentier. The fashion for chocolate was spread in France by Queen Maria Theresa, but before polite society discovered the pleasure of drinking it, it was used as a medicine.

Madame Victoire's Apartment

"Louis XV saw very little of his family; he went down to Madame Adélaïde's apartment each morning by a hidden staircase. He often brought and drank coffee that he had made himself. Madame Adélaïde would tug at a bell-pull, which would warn Madame Victoire of the King's visit; she told Madame Sophie, who would ring to warn Madame Louise." Madame Campan.

English Tea at the Prince de Conti's, by Barthélémy Ollivier. This painting shows the young Mozart during his 1766 visit to Paris. The young virtuoso made a great impression on Parisian salons, and was also received at Versailles by Louis XV.

Until the Revolution, the daughters of Louis XV lived in these apartments, which mostly look out onto the North Parterre. In the time of Louis XIV, this was the location of the sumptuous Bath Apartment, which was altered to make an apartment for Madame de Montespan, later granted to the Comtesse de Toulouse, and after her to Madame Pompadour. As part of the Museum of the History of France, they are now devoted to the Royal Family and the life of Society in the late eighteenth century.

Madame Adélaïde's Apartment

"Madame Adélaïde had an inordinate desire to learn; she learnt to play all the musical instruments from the horn (will people believe me?) to the Jew's harp."
Madame Campan.

Madame Adélaïde by Jean-Marc Nattier.

Madame Adélaïde's State Cabinet.

Marie-Antoinette's Apartment

In 1783, on the death of Madame Sophie, one of the daughters of Louis XV, Marie-Antoinette had a small apartment fitted out, giving onto the Marble Courtyard. It was next to the apartment of the Captain of the Guard at the foot of the King's Staircase.

Two paintings by Hubert Robert show the replanting of the park ordered by Louis XVI in 1774.

The Consulate and Empire Rooms

***Napoleon Addressing the 2nd Corps of the Grande Armée before the Attack on Augsburg*, by Claude Gautherat.**

There is no doubt that Versailles is the first museum of Napoleonic history. In his desire to reconcile all French political tendencies, Louis-Philippe devoted the whole of the ground floor of the South Wing to the Napoleonic era. In addition, since the reorganisation of the Museum at the turn of the century, the second-floor rooms above the Queen's Apartment (usually known as the Chimay Attic) and those on the second floor of the South Wing, running alongside the upper part of the Hall of Battles, are also devoted to the Consulate and the Empire. Apart from masterpieces by David and Gros, the visitor can also see sketches by Gérard, drawings by Dutertre, the paintings of Baron Lejeune and gouaches by Bagetti, which provide a colourful account of the Napoleonic period.

***General Bonaparte at the Pont d'Arcole on November 17th, 1796*, by Antoine-Jean Gros.**

Louis-Philippe and his Sons, by Horace Vernet.

The 19th-Century Rooms

The second floor of the North Wing is devoted to the events and public figures of the different regimes after the fall of Napoleon in 1815.

So much survives at Versailles from the time of Louis XIV and his two successors that it is easy to forget that the chateau also lived through the 19th century, which had a very difficult relationship to this symbol of absolute monarchy by divine right. Thus it was that Louis-Philippe, the citizen-King who emerged from the Revolution of 1830 and a descendant of Louis XIII, founded the Museum of the History of France, transforming Versailles into a focus for the national memory. This is why above the rooms maintained as they were in the 17th and 18th centuries there are rooms transformed under Louis-Philippe and devoted to the history of France.

The 17th-Century Rooms

The ground and first floors of the North Wing make a sort of preface to the tour of the royal apartments, and give a glimpse of France under the first three Bourbon kings.

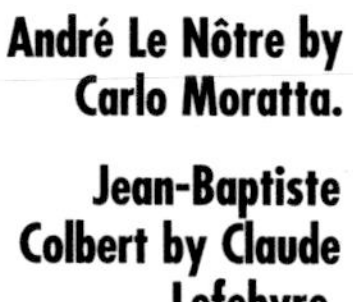

André Le Nôtre by Carlo Moratta.

Jean-Baptiste Colbert by Claude Lefebvre.

A view of the Chateau of Versailles in 1668 by Pierre Patel.

The Royal Opera

The architect Gabriel and the engineer Arnoult had planned a mechanism which would raise the floor of the auditorium to the same level as the stage, and it would then only be necessary to cover the pit to provide an enormous space for full-dress balls.

The shape of the opera-house, a truncated ellipse, was an innovation. It was built of wood for reasons of economy, and so as to provide excellent acoustics. In addition to the orchestra-pit, which can hold up to eighty musicians, and the stalls, there are three balcony levels whose raked arrangement gives a good view of the stage.

Music was always an important part of life at Versailles, and the birth of the French opera is closely linked to the reign of Louis XIV, so it is somewhat surprising that it was so long before the Opera was built. It was in fact on May 16, 1770, the day of the marriage of the Dauphin (the future Louis XVI) to Marie-Antoinette that the new opera-house was inaugurated. The first plans, though, had been commissioned from Hardouin-Mansart and Vigarani by Louis XIV in 1682, but wars and financial difficulties towards the end of his reign meant that it could not be built. The second design, presented by Gabriel to Louis XV in 1748, went through a long period of gestation, waiting twenty years before the King gave the order for work to begin.

When in 1661 the young Louis began to visit Versailles regularly, he was most interested at first in the gardens. To create something truly magnificent, he called on André Le Nôtre, whose work he knew from Fouquet's chateau at Vaux-le-Vicomte.

In 1664, the gardens were ready for the entertainment to be given by the King: *The Pleasures of the Enchanted Isle*. And in 1674, five days of festivities were organised to celebrate the second conquest of the Franche-Comté.

Despite constant problems of water-supply, the two Francine brothers, Florentine engineers, enabled Le Nôtre's layout to be completed with a multitude of fountains, cascades and other water-pieces.

3 The Water Parterre

The ponds of the Water Parterre are surrounded by bronze statues symbolising the main rivers of France, and others representing water-nymphs.

As Louis XIV advised in a guide he wrote himself (*The Manner of Presenting the Gardens of Versailles*), it is best to begin by descending the few steps from the terrace in front of the central facade, decorated with vases representing War, by Coysevox, and Peace, by Duby, to reach the Water Parterre. It consists of two enormous ponds dug in 1684-1685.

Below the Water Parterre, as Louis XIV suggests, one can "pause to consider Latona, the lizards, the ramps...". Drawing their inspiration from Ovid's *Metamorphoses*, the Marsy brothers, who made the sculptures for this fountain, illustrated the legend of the mother of Apollo and Diana. Seduced by Jupiter, Latona gave birth to the twins Apollo and Diana. But she was cursed by Jupiter's wife Juno. When the Marsy brothers installed their work in 1670, Latona and her children stood on a small rock, looking back towards the chateau, that is to say, towards the King. Around them are six Lycian peasants transformed into frogs. It was between 1687 and 1689 that Jules Hardouin-Mansart rearranged the fountain to give it its present appearance.

The Fountain of Latona 4

Below the steps, Latona and her twins Rude men low beasts are making for their sins, Transform them with the water that they throw: This one had hands where webbed feet now grow, Another stares, then feels hims elf mutate (...) The scene's a basin fair of vast extent, Around, the brood, degraded by th'event, With watery jets the gods attack in vain. La Fontaine, Les Amours de Psyche et de Cupidon.

13 The Royal Avenue

The Royal Avenue connects two fountains relating to the myth of Apollo: the birth of the God of the Sun is illustrated by the Fountain of Latona, and his course through the heavens by the Fountain of Apollo at the other end.

Although it was already laid out in the time of Louis XIII, it was Le Nôtre who gave the Royal Avenue its present size, 64 metres wide and 335 metres long. Also called the *Tapis Vert* or Green Carpet, the avenue is lined by twelve statues and twelve monumental vases copied from antique models by the pupils of the *Académie de France* in Rome.

Exhausted by the wanderings to which she had been condemned, Latona halts by the edge of a pond in Lycia, but the peasants refuse to allow her to drink, insulting her and polluting the water. She revenges herself by turning them into frogs.

The Fountain of Apollo 14

The lead sculpture executed by Tubi from designs by Le Brun shows Apollo in his chariot. The God of Light faces the chateau, that is to say, towards the King, and the rising sun.

The Apollo Fountain only took its name in 1671. There had been a circular pond on the same site under Louis XIII, which was dug in 1736 and called the *Bassin des Cygnes*, or Swan Pond. Beyond it stretches the Grand Canal, which was thirteen years in the making, 1,650 metres long and 62 metres wide and intersected by a transverse canal 1,013 metres in length. The King and courtiers would often take to the water in rowing-boats, or in the scaled-down ships that Louis XIV had brought from Marseille or Le Havre, or even in gondolas. These gondolas had been offered to Louis XIV by the Republic of Venice in 1674, together with four gondoliers who lived near the Grand Canal at a spot then called Little Venice.

In 1672 the area of the South Parterre was doubled by cutting down a grove of trees that lay to the west of the original parterre: the Green Wood. Le Nôtre was then able to organise it in two sections, each centred on a large circular pond. At that time it was called the Flower Parterre.

The South Parterre 1

The South Parterre lies beneath the windows of that part of the Chateau where the Royal family lived in the 18th century. It is overlooked on three sides by a terrace which offers a good view of the intricate tracery of flowers and bushes.

In winter, the Orangery sheltered nearly 3,000 orange-trees, lemon-trees, pomegranate-trees etc. which were brought out for the summer. Palm trees were introduced only in the 19th century.

This orangery, built by Jules Hardouin-Mansart between 1684 and 1686, replaced an older, much smaller orangery. The statue of the King in classical dress, commissioned from Desjardins by the Maréchal de la Feuillade, and offered by him to Louis XIV, was installed in the central niche in 1683. Its main gallery ends in the west with a small drawing room beneath a raised rotunda whose door opens onto the *Allée de Bacchus.*

The North Parterre contains some of the most beautiful sculpture in the Versailles gardens. Like its partner the South Parterre, it is made up of two symmetrical parts both organised around a pond, each of these decorated with sculptures of sirens and tritons. At the end of the central path is François Girardon's Pyramid Fountain, installed in 1679. One should also look at the sculptures which stand alongside the *Allée des Trois Fontaines*, which starts at the Water Parterre, passes the Evening Fountain, and then six statues from Colbert's great commission of 1674: Pierre Mazeline's *Europe*, Sybraique and Cornu's *Africa*, Raon's *Night*, Massou's *Earth* and Pierre Garnier's *Pastoral Poem*.

North Parterre:
The Pyramid
The Water Avenue
The Bathing Nymphs
The Dragon Fountain
The Neptune Fountain

The North Parterre 23

"One will then move on to the Pyramid and pause for a moment, and afterwards return to the chateau by way of the steps between the Knifegrinder and the kneeling Venus, turning around at the top of the steps to take in the North Parterre, the statues, the vases, the crowns, the Pyramid and what can be seen of Neptune, and then leaving the garden through the same door by which one entered it". This is how Louis XIV ends his tour of the Versailles gardens.

The Pyramid, done by Girardin from designs by Charles Le Brun.

Girardon's Bathing Nymphs.

The Water Avenue or *Allée des Marmousets.* The word "Marmouset" refers to the grotesque sculptures of young children, the work of Le Gros, Le Hongre, Lerambert, Mazeline and Buirette.

The central path of the North Parterre is continued as an avenue lined by fountains, supported by grotesque figures of children. The idea for these fountains was, apparently, Claude Perrault's (the architect of the Louvre Colonnade and of the Paris Observatory), who in 1670 had the first fourteen groups of children cast from the designs of Charles Le Brun. But before that, the visitor has to pass the fountain of the Bathing Nymphs, where one may admire the bas-reliefs, among them Giradon's famous *Nymphs of Diana Bathing.*

The Dragon Fountain depicts an episode from the myth of Apollo: Python, the legendary serpent killed by Apollo, is represented in monstrous form, surrounded by dolphins and cupids armed with bows and arrows.

The present sculptures are copies made in 1889, replacing the originals by the Marsy brothers. The engineers designed a mechanism which would shoot a jet of water as high as 27 metres from the dragon's mouth.

Built under Le Nôtre's direction between 1679 and 1681, the Neptune Fountain was completed in 1738 in the reign of Louis XV, when Jacques-Ange Gabriel made the final alterations. The group depicting Neptune and Amphitrite, the work of Adam Lambert-Sigisbert was installed two years later. The fountain was inaugurated by Louis XV on August 14, 1741, when those attending were able to admire its 99 jets.

The Neptune Fountain.

The *Bosquet des Rocailles*
The Queen's Grove
The Quincunxes
The *Salle des Marronniers*
The Mirror Pond and King's Garden
The Colonnade
The Fountains of Summer, Autumn and Winter
The *Bosquet des Dômes*
The Fountain of Enceladus
The Obelisk
The Baths of Apollo
The Fountain of Spring
The Children's Island

Away from the major axes of the gardens, the visitor will find the sometimes discreetly-hidden groves, which provided the background for the sumptuous entertainments.

Laid out between 1681 and 1683, under Louis XIV this grove was called the "Ball Room" on account of the marble dance-floor which used to occupy its centre. On festive evenings, the spectators would sit on the turf-covered steps of the amphitheatre. The musicians would stand above the cascade. The Queen's Grove as it is today was created by the painter Hubert Robert in 1774-1775, when the gardens were being replanted. It therefore corresponds not to Le Nôtre's idea of the formal French garden, but to the late 18th century's pronounced taste for the more informal "English" garden.

The South and North Quincunxes are decorated with marble terms, produced for Fouquet from drawings by Poussin by pupils of the *Académie de France* in Rome, and later purchased by Louis XIV.

The South Quincunx replaced the Candelabra Grove, and the North Quincunx the Dauphin's Grove.

On this site in 1673, Le Nôtre had created a maze with 39 fountains, each one of which illustrated a fable from Aesop, the inspirer of La Fontaine.

Dug in 1672, the Mirror Pond was part of a garden which included the Royal Island. When in the 19th century Louis XVIII asked the architect Dufour to restore Versailles, the latter replaced the Royal Island, which had become a swamp, with a garden of lawns and flower-beds which was given the name of King's Garden.

The *Salle des Marronniers* (Chestnut Hall) replaced the *Salle des Antiques*, which had been decorated with trimmed yew-trees and fountains alternately.

The King's Garden corresponds to the 18th-century taste for the "English" garden.

The Mirror Pond and Royal Island in 1688, by E. Allegrain.

The Colonnade designed by Jules Hardouin-Mansart, begun in 1685, was for a long time used for concerts.

Until 1685 the site of the present Colonnade was occupied by Le Nôtre's Grove of Springs with its narrow twisting paths weaving their way through the wood and crossing several little streams. On June 19, 1684, the Marquis de Dangeau noted in his diary that "the King has ordered a marble colonnade with big fountains for the spot where the Springs used to be". At the centre there now stands a copy of Girardon's *Rape of Persephone*.

Where the Fountains of Autumn, Spring and Summer now stand three temporary theatres were erected for the Grand Royal Entertainment given in 1668. The most spectacular was probably that built by Carlo Vigarani, where Lully and Molière's *Fêtes de l'Amour et de Bacchus* was performed. It had 1,200 seats, and the twelve-metre long stage was lit by 300 candles in crystal chandeliers.

Executed after drawings by Le Brun, the Fountains of Autumn and Winter are dedicated to Bacchus and Saturn, those of Spring and Summer to Flora and Ceres.

The Fountain of Autumn.

The Fountain of Winter .

The *Bosquet des Dômes* in 1688, by C. Simoneau the Younger.

In 1677-1678 Jules Hardouin-Mansart had built two pavilions which faced each other, and it is this which explains the name. Earlier, it had been called the Grove of Fame, from a statue which stood in the middle of the octagonal basin. It was moved in 1684, and two years later new sculptures were placed here which came from the Grotto of Tethys, destroyed during the building of the North Wing.

In 1671 Le Nôtre began work on a grove called the Council Chamber or Banquet Hall. It was transformed in 1704-1705 by Jules Hardouin-Mansart and was then called the Obelisk Grove. This is how Félibien describes the Council Chamber: "It is longer than it is wide; at the centre is an island surrounded by channels, with bridges at the two ends, which by a secret mechanism are made to advance or retreat to grant or deny entry. When the bridges are pulled back there are several jets of water which form something like a fence, and seventy-three other jets of equal height rise from many other places".

The centre of the Obelisk Pond is decorated with a clump of reeds from which spring some 230 jets of water to form an aquatic pyramid which can reach a height of 25 metres.

The sculptor Gaspard Marsy shows Enceladus, one of the Titans who in the myth attacked the gods of Olympus. Fleeing from Athena, he is buried beneath Etna.

Here, before the Baths of Apollo, stood the Swamp Pond, the idea of Madame de Montespan, according to Charles Perrault. There was "a tree from which sprang water through all its tin leaves, and reeds of the same stuff jetted water from every side."

The sculptures of *Apollo served by Nymphs* by Girardon and Regnandin, and the *Horses of the Sun* by Marsy and Guérin date from the reign of Louis XIV, and were originally intended for the Grotto of Thetys. The artificial grotto and present layout of the grove are the work of the painter Hubert Robert, in the reign of Louis XVI.

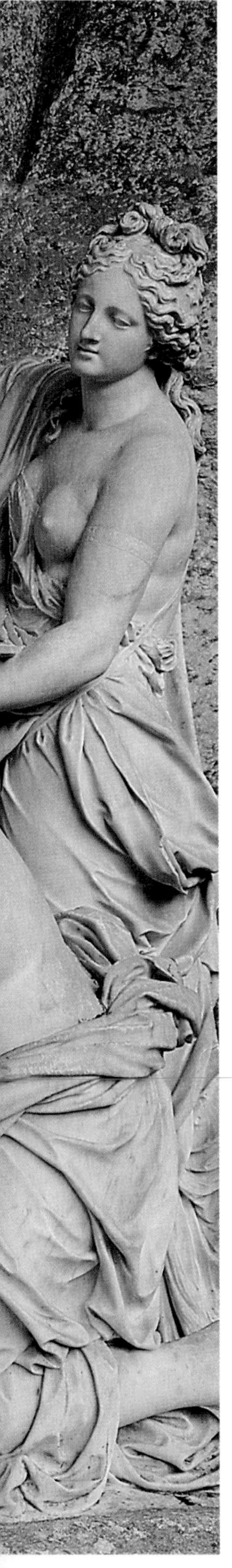

The Children's Island complemented the Water Theatre, of which nothing now remains. It consisted of a circular space surrounded by turfed steps, in which, as in many other groves, performances could be given. It was enlivened by four fountains decorated with groups of children and other water-pieces. The group now installed at the centre of the pond was sculpted by Hardy, and until 1710 it stood in the gardens of the first or "Porcelain" Trianon.

Hardy's Children's Island.

The Fountain of Spring.

The Fountain of Summer (opposite).

Trianon was the name of a village bought by Louis XIV in 1668 so as to use the site to build a pavilion for light refreshment. This pavilion, built by Le Vau in 1670, was decorated with white and blue tiles in imitation of Delft-ware, from which it got the name of Porcelain Trianon.
It was difficult to maintain and in 1687 threatened to fall into ruin, and the King decided to replace it with a proper chateau, in which it would be possible to live. So it was that Mansart built the chateau that we know today as the Grand Trianon, but which was then called the Marble Trianon from the way it was decorated.
The Trianon was for a long time neglected by Louis XV, but in 1750 he decided to have Madame de Maintenon's apartment redecorated for himself and Madame de Pompadour. Under Louis XVI, it was merely an annexe to the Petit Trianon.

The Grand Trianon

The Grand Trianon was intended to provide accommodation for the King, accompanied by no more than his family, a place of rest away from his official functions.

The Peristyle.

The Emperor's bedroom.
In the 19th century the Grand Trianon was occupied by Napoleon I, who intended it at first for his mother, but then used it himself, especially after his marriage to the Archduchess Marie-Louise. Louis-Philippe often came to stay there while work was being done to convert Versailles into a museum.

The Mirror Drawing Room.

"In the same way as in the chateau and the park at Versailles there are places where each season of the year seems to have found a particular home, it can be said that at the Trianon it is always Spring." Félibien, 1674.

Here at the Grand Trianon, as in all Louis XIV's other chateaux, the gardens play an important role. Although they were often altered, they retain the major divisions established at the time of the Porcelain Trianon (1670-1687) by the gardener Le Bouteux, the nephew of Le Nôtre. Seven steps lead from the Peristyle to the Upper Gardens, made up of two parterres each with a pond at the centre featuring a group of children by Girardon. Under Louis XIV the Lower Garden was planted with an abundance of orange-trees and fragrant flowers. The parterre is enlivened by an octagonal pond with a sculpture by Marsy of a child surrounded by grapes; its axis is prolonged by an avenue leading to the Mirror Fountain. To the south, a balustrade overlooks the horse-shoe pond beyond which lies the north branch of the Grand Canal.

The bedroom of the Queen of the Belgians.

Tour of the Grand Trianon

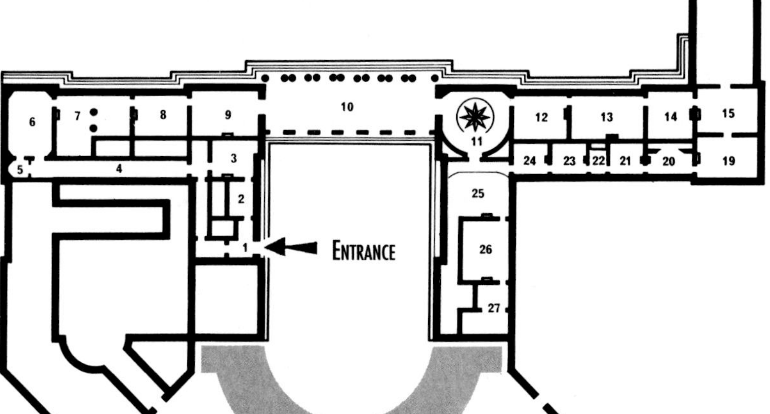

1 ● Vestibule
2 ● 1st Antechamber
3 ● 2nd Antechamber
4 ● Gallery
5 ● The Empress' Boudoir
6 ● Mirror Drawing Room
7 ● The Empress' Bedchamber
8 ● Chapel Antechamber
9 ● Courtiers' Drawing Room
10 ● Peristyle
11 ● *Salon Rond*
12 ● *Salon de Musique*
13 ● Louis-Philippe's Family Room
14 ● Sunset Cabinet or Malachite Room
15 ● Cool Drawing Room
16 ● Cotelle Gallery
17 ● Garden Drawing Room
18 ● Chapel
19 ● *Salon des Sources* or Emperor's Map Room
20 ● Sunrise Cabinet or Flowered Antechamber
21 ● The Emperor's Work Cabinet
22 ● Bathroom
23 ● The Emperor's Bedchamber
24 ● Breakfast Room
25 ● Games Room
26 ● Dining Room
27 ● Antechambers

The Petit Trianon

"A new kind of entertainment was given at the Petit Trianon. The art with which the English garden had not just been decorated with lights, but altogether lit up, produced a charming effect... there was not enough room for much of the court to enter; those who were not invited were unhappy, and the people, who pardon only entertainments they may enjoy themselves, had a great hand in the exaggerated ill-feeling about the costs of this little entertainment." Madame de Campan, *Memoirs*.

The Temple of Love.

In 1761 Gabriel built a small chateau, each facade of which is differently decorated, the richest being the one that gives onto the French Garden, with its Corinthian columns. The interior has largely remained as it was under Louis XV.

When Marie-Antoinette was given the Petit Trianon estate by Louis XVI she had rare plants brought from the King's Garden in Paris. She asked Hubert Robert, who was replanting the Versailles gardens at the time, and the architect Mique to redesign the grounds of her little estate. This was when the picturesque views, the streams and lawns that we still admire were created.

The buildings were planned little by little, often illustrating a fashion the Queen was following or inventing. In 1777, on a rock overlooking the lake, Mique built an octagonal pavilion called the Belvedere. At the same time, on the middle of an island visible from the Queen's bedroom, there was erected a classical temple, named the Temple of Love from the statue by Boudon which stands at its centre. In 1780 it was Mique again who built the theatre, in which Marie-Antoinette herself did not disdain to appear in such mildly scandalous productions as Beaumarchais' *Marriage of Figaro.*

Like his great-grandfather Louis XIV, Louis XV was a keen and well-informed lover of gardens, and it was in this spirit that in 1749 he had the north-eastern part of the Trianon estate laid out, later to be called the Petit Trianon. It was done in stages, starting with the construction of a new menagerie, followed by the design of a new parterre which they called the French Garden, in the centre of which in 1750 Gabriel built a pavilion, known as the French Pavilion. Further to the east, Louis XV asked the botanist Bernard de Jussieu to create a botanical garden, and put Claude Richard in charge of it. Nothing survives of this garden, where fig-trees and coffee-bushes were grown alongside geraniums and strawberries, nor of the great hothouse built in 1767.

Marie-Antoinette by Madame Vigée-Lebrun.

It was the Queen's Hamlet that made her garden famous. Like Madame de Lamballe at Rambouillet and the Condés at Chantilly, Marie-Antoinette wanted a village of her own, whose houses, modelled on the cottages of Normandy, in fact contained drawing-rooms of considerable elegance. Between 1783 and 1785 Mique built twelve houses, of which ten still stand, among them the Queen's Cottage, the Mill, and near the Dairy the Fishery or Marlborough Tower.

THE QUEEN'S HAMLET

The hamlet was a real little farm where Marie-Antoinette came to amuse herself; Madame Campan writes that she "took pleasure in running around all the buildings, watching the cows being milked and fishing in the lake."

The Mill.

The Queen's Cottage.

Achevé d'imprimer le 15 décembre 1997
par HÉRISSEY - France
Dépôt légal décembre 1997
ISBN 2-85495-061-5